4-8-2022

Sister step.
I hope
you....
Love your Bro. in
christ Jesus.
JAMES

Especially for

....

From

....

Date

....

Just
Between
Us,
God

Just Between Us, God

A Devotional Journal

BARBOUR BOOKS
An Imprint of Barbour Publishing, Inc.

Published by Barbour Books, an imprint of Barbour Publishing, Inc., 1810 Barbour Drive, Uhrichsville, Ohio 44683, www.barbourbooks.com

Our mission is to inspire the world with the life-changing message of the Bible.

 Member of the
Evangelical Christian
Publishers Association

Printed in China.

Just between You and God!

These more than ninety inspiring devotions, alongside related journal prompts and generous writing space, will encourage you to record your personal thoughts directed toward the heavenly Father.

Each devotion, rooted in scripture and written from Christ's heavenly perspective, will leave you feeling perfectly loved and blessed. And, with each turn of the page, you'll delight in an ongoing conversation—just between your heart and God's!

*God made my life complete when I placed all
the pieces before him. When I got my act together,
he gave me a fresh start. Now I'm alert to God's ways;
I don't take God for granted. Every day I review the
ways he works; I try not to miss a trick. I feel put back
together, and I'm watching my step. God rewrote
the text of my life when I opened the book
of my heart to his eyes.*
PSALM 18:20–24 MSG

Above All Else

"Steep your life in God-reality, God-initiative, God-provisions. Don't worry about missing out. You'll find all your everyday human concerns will be met."
MATTHEW 6:33 MSG

You may be wondering why life can seem so hard sometimes; why you keep falling into the trap of fear, worry, and angst; why the world seems to be so upside down. It is because you are not seeking Me above everything else.

Each morning before your feet hit the floor, spend time with Me. Come into My presence and peace. Allow Me to fill your heart with My love, so much so that it will spill out onto those whose lives you touch.

Determine to view the world through My eyes, to see the light of God in each and every person. Rest in the assurance that all is well. I have laid out a perfect path for you. To find your way, you simply have to stop and ask directions. Be certain that no matter what happens, I am beside you. In My hand is everything you will ever need. Trust. Hope. Relax. Know that I am with you every step of the way.

Above all else in heaven and on earth, seek first My Kingdom and My way of doing things, and everything else will fall into place.

Father God, I want to seek You above all. . .

_____
_____
_____
_____
_____
_____
_____
_____
_____
_____
_____
_____
_____
_____
_____
_____
_____
_____
_____
_____
_____
_____
_____

Spiritual Eyes

*"For we have no power against this great multitude
that is coming against us; nor do we know what
to do, but our eyes are upon You."*
2 CHRONICLES 20:12 NKJV

In these moments with Me, gently close your eyes. Envision My presence beside you. Feel My breath upon your face. Bask in the warmth of My light. Your inner eyes are upon Me. Here there is no reason to fear or fret. In your powerlessness, you feel My strength. Breathe easy. Then commit these moments to memory.

In this power, in this memory, reopen your eyes. I am still with you—and always will be no matter what you face today. Don't worry about anything. Simply keep your spiritual eyes on Me. Know that I will never let anything harm you. Know that I will always be with you. Know that you don't have to always have the answer. Look to Me for all wisdom, strength, and power. For all I have is yours. And I have promised I will always be here for you.

Thus, you may this day and all days walk forward in victory, no matter who or what is coming against you. Rest in My might, with your eyes upon Me. For in Me lie all answers.

Lord Jesus, I want to feel Your presence today. . .

_____

_____

_____

_____

_____

_____

_____

_____

_____

_____

_____

_____

_____

_____

_____

_____

_____

_____

_____

_____

_____

_____

_____

Miracle Maker

*And he did not do many miracles
there because of their lack of faith.*
MATTHEW 13:58 NIV

Woman, I am ready to do so many miracles in your life. Do you believe Me?

The greater your faith in Me, the more amazing things I can do in your life and in the lives of those around you. Do not limit Me. Train yourself to think outside the box. Humble yourself enough to believe in My grandeur. Push your doubts aside. Remember that I am the One who changed water into wine, healed lepers, calmed the sea and wind, and rose from the dead. There is nothing I *cannot* do—if your faith is big enough.

And once the miracle begins, it will continue for as long as you keep your eyes on Me. So do not look away, or you may sink down into the sea of doubt.

You are a woman of amazing strength. There is no door closed to one who believes in the impossible. And that's My art—to make the impossible possible. Will you help Me? Will you not doubt? Will you believe anything can happen? If so, pray and petition. Watch and wait. Then praise and repeat.

Almighty Father, I believe. . .

Know Me

*"Before I shaped you in the womb, I knew all about you.
Before you saw the light of day, I had holy plans for you."*
JEREMIAH 1:5 MSG

I see you as no one else does. Your face, your hands, your size, your shape, your hair, your breath, your sigh—all these I know intimately. To Me, you are no stranger but an extension, an expression of Myself as you move in the light of love, forgiveness, and charity.

Yet at times, it seems I am yet a stranger to you. This will not do.

When you are worshipping or praying to Me, you cannot help but feel My love. Yet when you leave My presence, you sometimes leave Me and My love behind. My light and love are for you not just to experience in a moment of devotion but to carry back out into the world. How else will the world around you be changed?

So, friend and daughter, seek Me out daily. Feel the peace of My presence. Bask in the light of My love. Listen to the sound of My breath and My sigh. See Me as you have never seen Me before. Then take Me with you, out into the world. Become an extension of Me. Forgive the seemingly unforgivable. Love the unlovable. Help the helpless.

In doing so, you will begin to know Me as I know you—forever and ever, amen.

I want to know You, Lord. . .

Working Out a Way

Hannah prayed: I'm bursting with God-news! I'm walking on air. I'm laughing at my rivals. I'm dancing my salvation. Nothing and no one is holy like God, no rock mountain like our God. Don't dare talk pretentiously—not a word of boasting, ever! For God knows what's going on. He takes the measure of everything that happens.
1 Samuel 2:1–5 msg

I see all. I know exactly what your heart desires. Yet I would have the words of your wants come to Me by your own lips. Tell Me exactly what you want. Show Me exactly what you desire. And I, in return, will answer your prayer in accordance with My wisdom.

You see, I see all things—not just your desires but those of all My children. Like a child, you may desire something that may not be good for you today, but perhaps it will be tomorrow. So be patient. Continually pare down your focus to what you truly desire with all of your mind, body, heart, and soul. And if it would be good for you and the world, your desire shall be granted.

Simply leave all in My hands and go forward, knowing your Father will only give you what is good and right for you in this time and space. And in the meantime, be content, knowing that I am working out a way for you to be all I created you to be—nothing more and nothing less than spectacular today and every day!

Heavenly Father, I leave it all in Your capable hands. . .

Pure Joy

Light is sown for the [uncompromisingly] righteous and strewn along their pathway, and joy for the upright in heart [the irrepressible joy which comes from consciousness of His favor and protection].
PSALM 97:11 AMPC

I am your Rock. Your Fortress. Your solid foundation! Do you see this?

When you come to Me, you seem to know Me. You recognize who I am and what I have done for you. But when you finish your prayers or devotion, you seem to leave Me where I am and try to live life in your own power! This shall not do!

Do you want joy? Do you want peace? Do you want strength? Do you want power? Then, My dear woman, remember that I am always looking out for you! I am always standing by your side! I see what you see—and so much more! So keep Me close. So close that you can hear Me breathe in rhythm with you. So close that you can hear Me whisper. So close that you can feel My power surging through you.

Knowing that I am with you, that I am anxious to bless you, and that I am shielding you with all that I am will give you all the joy you could want—so much that it spills over you and onto others who may not yet know Me. With Me *truly* in your life and the *light* of your life, your pure joy cannot help but run over!

Father God, with You in my life. . .

Streaming Thoughts

You will guard him and keep him in perfect and constant peace whose mind [both its inclination and its character] is stayed on You, because he commits himself to You, leans on You, and hopes confidently in You.
ISAIAH 26:3 AMPC

You must train yourself, My child, to be a witness to the thoughts that are streaming through your head. The negative thoughts are only shadows of reality, mucking up your mind. Do not let them have sway or power over you. Instead, let them flow through unheeded. Pay no attention to the fear, panic, hatred, lust, grief, and aggression they bring with them. Just allow them to pass away. If more strength is needed, simply call on Me. When you say My name, "Jesus," My light makes all shadows disperse. All evil fades. For it has no strength, no power against Me.

Just keep your mind on Me. Hand over your entire self—mind, body, spirit, soul. I will keep you safe from all harm. I will give you all the joy and strength you need. You need not look anywhere else.

Feed on Me, your Bread of life. Drink of Me, your Living Water Come to Me, your Burden Bearer, eternal Friend, Light of the World. Rest assured that I will never leave you, fail you, forsake you. And that's the truth. That's My promise and your confidence.

In Your name, God, there is power. . .

Always Present

*"Look!" he answered, "I see four men loose,
walking in the midst of the fire; and they are not hurt,
and the form of the fourth is like the Son of God."*

DANIEL 3:25 NKJV

You have had your sorrows and temptations in this life as well as heartbreak, rejection, and derision. And through it all, whether you knew it or not, whether you recognized Me or not, I was walking with you.

In the midst of your fire, I felt the flame. In the midst of your flood, I felt the undercurrent. In the midst of your earthquake, I felt the earth tremble.

No matter where you are, no matter what happens, I am walking this road with you. So stop. Take a rest. Call My name—and then you will see Me. Then you will know that I've been right next to you all along.

Thus there is no reason to dread the fire, flood, or earthquakes in your life. There is no reason to let them shake you up. You can be confident in Me, My presence, My strength. I am holding on to you tightly and will never, ever, ever let you go. Simply put your hand in Mine, and walk on. The Son of God is walking with you.

In Your presence, Lord, I am confident. . .

Love—Pure and Unfettered

But God showed his great love for us by sending
Christ to die for us while we were still sinners.

ROMANS 5:8 NLT

There are some things (and some people) you may never be able to change. But that is not your affair. Your business is loving all—no matter who they are or what they do. For didn't I love you when you were still somewhat confused or ignorant of My presence and My ways?

The best way to show others the Way is to shower them with the love you get from Me. That's why I've asked you to feed the hungry, clothe the naked, visit the prisoner. While you are at it, do something nice for the intrusive mother-in-law, the demanding boss, the unfriendly neighbor, the gum-cracking checkout girl, the desperate-looking homeless man. Find a way to reach the heart of others by tapping into My reserves. Each kindness you bestow upon another restores My reserves *and* comes back at you a hundredfold.

So don't let others irritate. Instead allow them to help you navigate your way through this world. Let them be markers on your road to paradise. Let them see our love for what it is—pure and unfettered.

Who can you bless this way? Who can you love today?

Heavenly Father, show me how to love better. . .

The Light

Let be and be still, and know
(recognize and understand) that I am God.
PSALM 46:10 AMPC

Rest your body. Sit back in your chair. Put your feet flat on the floor. Relax. Allow My light and life to fill you from the top of your head to the bottom of your feet.

Breathe easy. One breath, then two, then three. Let all the troubles of the world fade away. Whatever has happened, has happened. Whatever will be, will be. Let it go. Drift away from the earthly world. Rise up to the Kingdom of God.

Come to Me now. In My presence there is peace. Here you are surrounded by a love that can never die. Here there is no sorrow or pain. There is only a light that glows like no other. It is the light of a life with Me.

You too can have this light. It's a light that you can shine into the earthly world. It's a light that will point others to Me. Let this light shine. Let it fill you to overflowing. Let it lead you to all good things.

Rest here for a moment or two longer. Then, as you slowly return to the earthly world, remember the light that you have within. Keep the flame alive by spreading My love. Keep the darkness at bay. Be still. Know that I am God—and that you are the light of this world.

Lord, I want to be still. . .

The Remedy

But you have come to Mount Zion, to the city of the living God,
the heavenly Jerusalem. You have come to thousands upon
thousands of angels in joyful assembly. . . . You have come to
God, the Judge of all. . .to Jesus the mediator of a new covenant.
HEBREWS 12:22–24 NIV

Gently, gently lift your head. There is no sorrow so deep that I cannot heal it. No pain so great I cannot remedy it. Come to Me. Put your *entire* self—not just your mind or just your body, but your mind, body, soul, and spirit—in My hands. Release from yourself any distrust, doubt, and despair as air from a balloon, until there is no debility remaining that would hinder My work, until there is nothing left but a foundation of freedom, a time of rest, and a spark of hope. Then allow Me to build you back up as you abide in Me and My Spirit abides in you. I am your Healer. I am your remedy. I am the answer to all of your questions. Remain in this secret place with Me. Know that I am the greatest and mightiest force in heaven and on earth. With Me you are vulnerable, yet safe; you are home, yet a foreigner in a strange place; you are alone, yet surrounded by Myself and a heavenly host.

Heavenly Healer, thank You for. . .

From Dawn to Dusk

What a beautiful thing, GOD, to give thanks, to sing an anthem
to you, the High God! To announce your love each daybreak,
sing your faithful presence all through the night.
PSALM 92:1–2 MSG

Do not be a stranger. As the day breaks, come into My presence. Then linger with Me for a moment. Allow Me to be your morning provision. I am—and have—all you need to face each and every day. If given the opportunity, I will richly nourish your spirit, strengthen your body, spark your mind, and gladden your soul. All this I, the Risen Son, will give you before you step one foot on the ground. It is a feast treasured by many saved souls.

So do not bypass these precious moments. Come. Linger. Open yourself to My supply that will fortify you throughout your day.

And then when day is done, the sun has set, come to Me once again. Do not be afraid of the darkness. There is no shadow that can separate us. So lay yourself down. Breathe easy upon your bed. Envision Me beside you once more. Thank Me for the countless blessings you received from My hand. Say a prayer for your family and friends. Then enter the sleep of the innocent. And may your gentle smile be the precursor to the joy of the dreams you are about to witness.

Today I come into Your presence, Father. . .

Dreams

Commit your way to the Lord [roll and repose each care of your load on Him]; trust (lean on, rely on, and be confident) also in Him and He will bring it to pass.
PSALM 37:5 AMPC

Why do you continue to try and do everything in your own power? Why do you not ask Me for advice, direction, help? You act as if I am to have no part in helping your dreams come true. Or that you need to carry all the burden of attaining your dream on your own shoulders, as if your strength is the end-all and be-all. Instead of carrying this entire load by yourself, come to Me. Tell Me what your dreams and aspirations are—and why. Lay them in My tender hands. Then rest well in the knowledge that I will enlighten you. That I will give you the wisdom to make the right decisions, to take the right path. I will help you to determine what is best for your life—as well as the people in it. When you bare your heart before Me, when you tell Me everything that is on your mind, when you open up to Me like no other, I cannot help but be moved. So don't hold back. Tell Me all, and I will help you make all your dreams a reality!

Dream-Giver, I ask for Your direction. . .

First Come, Always Served

*What sorrow awaits those who look to Egypt for help,
trusting their horses, chariots, and charioteers and
depending on the strength of human armies instead
of looking to the LORD, the Holy One of Israel.*

ISAIAH 31:1 NLT

Where are you looking for help? To things, other people, money, or institutions? Don't you know that they are all fallible? That none of them are unchangeable, eternal, and filled with the awesome power of God? Do you not know the only thing that can truly save you is Myself?

Look to Me—and Me alone for each and every need! Even though getting you out of the pit *seems* impossible, nothing is too difficult for Me! Can you not wait for Me to rescue you in My own timing? Don't look for other "things" to save you right here and now. Be patient! I have bigger plans in mind for you.

Do you need something to believe in? Don't fall for that false American idol. Look to Me. Do you need or want a man in your life? Don't give yourself to every Tom, Dick, and Harry, but give yourself more fully to Me. Do you need financial help? Come to Me. Have faith that I will provide. Do you need employment? Checking the want ads is fine, but come to Me first. I will open doors you had no clue even existed.

Look to Me before all things, believe in My power—and watch great plans unfold! When you consistently come first to Me, you will always be served!

Unchanging God, I look to You. . .

Word Power

For the Word that God speaks is alive and full of power [making it active, operative, energizing, and effective]; it is sharper than any two-edged sword, penetrating to the dividing line of the breath of life (soul) and [the immortal] spirit, and of joints and marrow [of the deepest parts of our nature], exposing and sifting and analyzing and judging the very thoughts and purposes of the heart.
HEBREWS 4:12 AMPC

So you were going along fine, and then you read something in My Word that has stopped you in your tracks. My daughter, this is a good thing! This Word that you read each and every day is alive! It is speaking directly to your soul! It reaches where nothing else can! It is pointing out something in your life that you need to address. Perhaps there is a friend or neighbor you need to apologize to, a wrong you have been avoiding but need to right. Perhaps there is a child or a younger woman looking for guidance, hope, and direction. Perhaps you have been storing more treasures on earth than in heaven and priorities need to be shifted. Perhaps it is something that goes much deeper, something you cannot quite discern. In each of these cases, there is a reason to praise! I am speaking directly to your life!

I and the Word—one and the same—are indeed alive, leading you, guiding you, helping you. Spend some more time in meditation with Me today. Apply to My wisdom. Ask, seek, knock—then you will know and all things will be set right.

Father God, Your Word speaks volumes to my heart. . .

Overflowing Blessings

Bring all the tithes (the whole tenth of your income) into the storehouse, that there may be food in My house, and prove Me now by it, says the Lord of hosts, if I will not open the windows of heaven for you and pour you out a blessing, that there shall not be room enough to receive it.

MALACHI 3:10 AMPC

You are like every good woman, oftentimes driven to nurture and do for others before nurturing or doing for yourself. Yet living thus may weaken you, not only physically, mentally, and emotionally but spiritually as well. Take this moment to reevaluate your life. Come before Me and be totally honest. Where are you giving most of yourself—to your job, your family, your friends, your education, your church? If so, stop. Reconsider.

Give your all first to Me, your Lord and Savior. Bring all your tithes—your talents, hopes, dreams, love, passion, gifts, mind, soul, spirit—to Me. Put them in My possession. Trust Me with all that you are, have, and ever hope to be. Then see what happens!

Watch how the windows of heaven will open and pour blessing upon blessing into your life. Let go of all you are holding on to—doubts, worries, fears, possessions, money, jealousies, nightmares, anger, confusion, fear, memories, grief, stress, feelings of unworthiness—so that you can open up your hands to capture all the gifts I am bursting to give you. Give to Me until I overflow onto you.

Heavenly Father, today I give You. . .

A Stretch of Faith

Then Jesus said to the centurion, "Go! Let it be done just as you believed it would." And his servant was healed at that moment.

MATTHEW 8:13 NIV

I, Jesus Christ, can do anything, for I am God's one and only Son. So why is it that, at times, you limit Me? If only you had the faith of the commander I met thousands of years ago. He desired healing for his servant boy. That in itself is commendable, that this centurion would come and chase Me down for a blessing for a young servant. But what was even more commendable was that he said all I had to do was say the word—and he knew the boy would be cured!

Do you have that faith? Do you trust that all I have to do is say the word and what you believe will be done—in the twinkling of an eye? When I was walking among you, God in the form of flesh, I healed many, many people of illness. I walked on water. I calmed the sea and the wind. I turned water into wine. I made the blind to see, the lame to walk. I withered a fig tree with mere words. When My disciples saw it, they marveled. And My words to them are the same words I am now saying to you: "Have a constant faith in God. And whatever you believe will take place will be done." The same goes for you, woman. Constantly be stretching your faith and watch amazing things unfold.

Lord Jesus, I don't want to place limits on You. . .

Refuge

*The name of the Lord is a strong tower; the [consistently]
righteous man [upright and in right standing with God]
runs into it and is safe, high [above evil] and strong.*
PROVERBS 18:10 AMPC

When you are sore and weary, run to Me. When you are tired of your frantic pace, run to Me. When you are frightened, confused, and overwhelmed by the darkness of this world, run to Me. When you can no longer read My Word through your tears, run to Me. When you feel that all is lost and you can no longer go on, run to Me—for I AM.

I am all the nourishment you need, for I am your living water and miraculous manna. I am all the protection you need, for I am your breastplate. I am all the comfort you could want, for no shoulder is bigger than Mine. I, your strong tower, am your shelter in the mightiest of storms. Here in My presence, no evil can touch you. Nothing can penetrate My shield of love for the people who are called by My name.

So in your time of trial, turn to no one but Me. And you will rest secure in My everlasting arm that is never too short to pull you out of danger and into My protective hold. Come. Abide in Me as I abide in My Father. Here you may rest. Here you will come to no harm. Here you shall remain until you have been restored and are ready to go on.

Nourisher and Protector, I run to You. . .

The Wisdom of God

To those whom God has called, both Jews and Greeks,
Christ the power of God and the wisdom of God. For the
foolishness of God is wiser than human wisdom, and the
weakness of God is stronger than human strength.
1 CORINTHIANS 1:24–25 NIV

Do not lose hope and faith if you are mocked or called foolish because of your belief in Me and My Word. Even My disciples had trouble totally understanding what I was doing while on earth. When told I had risen again, the eleven thought the words of the women were nonsense. But that did not take away the power and effect of the truth of the matter. And I am the way, the life, and the truth. All of My Word reveals the power of God. It brings to light His wisdom—even though it seems like foolishness to the world of men.

Know that even if your mind cannot understand the who, what, when, where, why, and how of the Gospel and all that preceded it, it matters not. For God, through Me and My Word, has saved, is saving, and will save all who believe in Me. He has made each one of you His daughter through faith in Me. What else is there to know? Simply believe in the Word. Believe in its power. And as you continue to walk with God, Me, and the Holy Spirit, your life will, in the eyes of this foolish world, become an extraordinary example of the supernatural power of God.

Thank You for saving me, Father. . .

Quietness and Confidence

For thus said the Lord God, the Holy One of Israel:
In returning [to Me] and resting [in Me] you shall be saved;
in quietness and in [trusting] confidence shall be your strength.
ISAIAH 30:15 AMPC

How many times will you seek to do things in your own power before coming to Me for help? How often will you find yourself stressed out because you've forgotten where your true strength comes from? Yes, you are human. But you also have the light of God within you. You need to feed that fire by spending time with Me and in My Word. So stop running hither and yon, looking for answers, joy, and purpose in earthly wisdom and material possessions. Take a few moments to rest in Me, to be recharged in My power, to regain your strength.

Only I can give you the peace you need. Only I can calm your heart within so you can face the world without. Only I can give you the confidence to accomplish all you have been created to do. Only I can give you the wisdom to live a heavenly life on earth. So slow your steps. Remember and revel in your complete dependence upon Me. Then, and only then, will true joy fill your heart and the flame of your spirit light up the darkness in this world.

I can't do this alone, Lord Jesus. . .

Safety Net

*In peace I will both lie down and sleep, for You, Lord,
alone make me dwell in safety and confident trust.*
PSALM 4:8 AMPC

I alone am the answer to your worries. I alone can give you true peace. When you are fraught with worries, come into My presence. Speak My healing Words to soothe your heart and spirit. Continually repeat, "Jesus is with me. All is well."

I can help you—and your loved ones—in any situation. I can not only save you spiritually but keep you safe physically. You need run to no other place but My arms. I am your shepherd, willing to carry you, to die for you, to lead you, to heal you. I stand between you and the evil, the wolves of this world. With My staff and My rod ready to guide and protect you, you can rest easy. This peace, this confidence that only I can give you cannot be bought. It is fully and freely given—from My heart to yours, from My spirit to yours, from My mind to yours, from My soul to yours. Expect nothing less in the hours between sunset and sunrise. Bask in My peace. Slumber in My presence. Take that great leap of faith, for I am your safety net, on earth and in heaven.

Because of You, Lord, it is well. . .

Sweet Forgiveness

Then Peter came to Him and said, "Lord, how often shall my brother sin against me, and I forgive him? Up to seven times?" Jesus said to him, "I do not say to you, up to seven times, but up to seventy times seven."

MATTHEW 18:21–22 NKJV

What is wonderful and humbling about forgiveness is not just giving it—but asking for it. When you come to Me, your heart in your hand, asking My forgiveness, it touches My heart, deep down. For in this desire for forgiveness, in this act of humility, you are closest to My Spirit.

It is the same feeling that a mother gets when her child humbly comes into her presence, eyes down on the ground, feet shuffling, and tells her he broke her favorite china cup. Her tears cannot help but well up in her eyes as the mother sees the sincere remorsefulness and sorrow in her son's face. And, as the years pass, wouldn't it be a wonderful lesson for him if she herself humbly asked him for forgiveness when she does him a wrong?

Forgiveness is sweet. And if it can be granted by Me to you all the years of your life, you shall be able to grant it to all those who wrong you—even if it takes 490 times.

I *need* Your forgiveness, Father. . .

Like a Child

[Jesus] said, Truly I say to you, unless you repent (change, turn about) and become like little children [trusting, lowly, loving, forgiving], you can never enter the kingdom of heaven [at all]. Whoever will humble himself therefore and become like this little child [trusting, lowly, loving, forgiving] is greatest in the kingdom of heaven.

MATTHEW 18:3–4 AMPC

Where is the joyful innocence you once had? Where have the easy spirit, the trusting nature, the curious mind, the happy exuberance, and the enthusiasm gone? Do not let this world's shadows overcome your light. Do not let its wisdom drown out your spiritual intuition and discernment. Do not let its dog-eat-dog and it's-all-about-me attitude sweep you up in its embrace.

Instead, go against the worldly current by riding in the boat with Me. There will be times of storm, where the winds and the waves threaten to capsize your vessel. But with Me in the boat, you will never sink down into the depths but will walk on the water and someday rise up to paradise to be with Me. Heaven is the only true kingdom to aspire to, for it will still be there when all the earthly kingdoms fall away.

So live this life with Me in joy! Trust and keep on trusting. Forgive and be forgiven. Love and be loved. Laugh, love, leap—and sing to the Lord a new song, the one you've kept hidden in your childlike heart.

Almighty Father, grow my trust. . .

....

....

....

....

....

....

....

....

....

....

....

....

....

....

....

....

....

....

....

....

....

....

....

....

....

....

....

No More Fetters

Those who wait for the Lord [who expect, look for, and hope in Him] shall change and renew their strength and power; they shall lift their wings and mount up [close to God] as eagles [mount up to the sun]; they shall run and not be weary, they shall walk and not faint or become tired.
ISAIAH 40:31 AMPC

You are a woman with amazing opportunities. When you take your eyes off the ground and look up with a God perspective, there is nothing you cannot do. Hope in Me. Wait for My timing. Expect good things to happen. Instead of seeing yourself as a limited being, cut away the fetters of your mind. Break the chain that binds you to self-limiting beliefs.

You have My resurrection power. You have My strength and protection. You have the Holy Spirit's wisdom and direction. Soar as you were divinely designed to do. Rise above pride, pettiness, selfishness, self-absorption, greed, narrow-mindedness, and fear. Break away from the comfort of the ordinary and seek out a new world, the one I am calling you to. And as you rise, as you mount up to the sun, you will find Me becoming clearer and clearer. In My strength, you will not grow tired but find each updraft taking you higher and higher into My will. Wait. Expect. Change. And mount up. In My power, you will soar.

Lord Jesus, I want to rise. . .

Amazing Praise

As they began to sing and praise, the Lord set ambushes against the men of Ammon and Moab and Mount Seir who were invading Judah, and they were defeated. . . . So Jehoshaphat and his men went to carry off their plunder, and they found among them a great amount of equipment and clothing and also articles of value— more than they could take away.
2 Chronicles 20:22, 25 NIV

When you face trouble, praise. When you are filled with fear, praise. When you are threatened and are uncertain of what to do, praise. When you need help from Me, praise. When you are discouraged, praise. When you meet the enemy face-to-face, praise. Lift up your head, seek My face, look for My light, then praise My name in a very loud voice: "Give thanks to the Lord! His amazing love lasts forever! He is the First and the Last! He is unchangeable! He is undefeatable! With Him in my life, no man or woman can harm me."

With such a mind-set, such a statement emanating from your lips, you will have victory—such victory that you will not be able to carry all the blessings you gain at My hand. Such amazing praise, such a firm assurance in Me and My promises, cannot help but result in triumph!

Heavenly Father, I will be victorious because. . .

The Crazy Law of Love

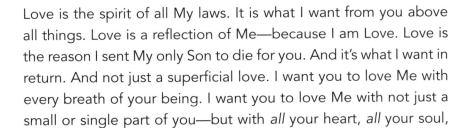

" 'Love the Lord your God with all your passion and prayer
and intelligence'. . . . 'Love others as well as you love
yourself.' These two commands are pegs; everything in
God's Law and the Prophets hangs from them."
MATTHEW 22:37–40 MSG

Love is the spirit of all My laws. It is what I want from you above all things. Love is a reflection of Me—because I am Love. Love is the reason I sent My only Son to die for you. And it's what I want in return. And not just a superficial love. I want you to love Me with every breath of your being. I want you to love Me with not just a small or single part of you—but with *all* your heart, *all* your soul, and *all* your mind. And not just a sometime love—but an all-day, everyday love with no holds barred! That's the first part.

The second part goes along with it. I want you to love all others as you love yourself. That means respecting yourself. Looking out for the good of your own soul—as well of those souls of everyone else on earth, whether they have been good to you or not. I want you to be a constant giver of love, whether or not it is deserving. When you were not deserving, I sacrificed My Son for you. Does it not make sense then that I would want you to love others, regardless of whether it is deserved? Now that's crazy—but that's love!

Lover of my soul, You are the reason. . .

Overflowing with Hope

*May the God of hope fill you with all joy and peace
as you trust in him, so that you may overflow
with hope by the power of the Holy Spirit.*
ROMANS 15:13 NIV

Do you want the peace that surpasses all understanding? Then empty yourself of all worldly angst and worry. Put all your trust in Me. I am the One who can give you that amazing calmness, the One who can help you sleep peacefully in the midst of a boat-rocking storm. This wonderful peace is a precursor to all-encompassing joy. And this joy and peace lead to an overabundance of hope!

It's available through the power of the Helper I sent to you thousands of years ago. That same power has not abated. That power was available to miracle workers of old—and is still available to you today. The same amount. The same strength. And you are the vessel for that power. All you need to do is trust Me, reach out, believe in Me, and I will fill you to overflowing with hope—all you need to lead a victorious life in Me. My greatest desire for you is that you live this blessed life to the fullest. Are you ready to have your cup running over?

Heavenly Father, my cup runneth over. . .

The Word

*In the beginning [before all time] was the Word (Christ),
and the Word was with God, and the Word was God Himself.
He was present originally with God. All things were made
and came into existence through Him; and without Him
was not even one thing made that has come into being.*

JOHN 1:1–3 AMPC

I have been around since the very beginning of time. I spoke things into being. Through Me, the world was made. For nothing was made until I spoke it into existence. And with the help of the Holy Spirit, I continue to make My thoughts clear to you through the written Word—that Bible you have before you. The precious book you hold in your hands.

As you read the Word, study it, and apply it to your life, you find yourself drawing closer and closer to Me. The Word in action makes you more and more like Me. This Word is power. This Word is truth. This Word is the answer to every question you have in life. Take it to heart, for nothing is more precious, more powerful, and more perfect.

Father God, Your Word is precious to me. . .

_____

_____

_____

_____

_____

_____

_____

_____

_____

_____

_____

_____

_____

_____

_____

_____

_____

_____

_____

_____

_____

_____

_____

_____

_____

Ready Help

Now that we know what we have—Jesus, this great High Priest with ready access to God—let's not let it slip through our fingers. We don't have a priest who is out of touch with our reality. He's been through weakness and testing, experienced it all—all but the sin. So let's walk right up to him and get what he is so ready to give. Take the mercy, accept the help.

HEBREWS 4:14–16 MSG

I know all that is going on in your life. So please, do not try to hide yourself away. Instead, bring all your shame and troubles to Me. I am so ready to lift you above all your sorrows. I too have lived in your world. I have felt the pain and affliction it can bring. But I have also experienced the world's joys and triumphs.

So let go of all the chains that keep you from coming to Me. Break through all the self-made barriers that would have you cower in the dark. Step out of that dungeon and into the light of My presence. Walk right up and take what I am ready to give you. I have more mercy, love, kindness, and strength than you could ever imagine. And there is no one I would rather help than you, no one I would rather lift up than you, and no one I would rather love than you, for I see who you really are and who you are about to be.

Lift me up, Lord. . .

....

....

....

....

....

....

....

....

....

....

....

....

....

....

....

....

....

....

....

....

....

....

Certain as the Dawn

Come and let us return to the Lord. . . . Yes, let us know
(recognize, be acquainted with, and understand) Him;
let us be zealous to know the Lord [to appreciate, give heed
to, and cherish Him]. His going forth is prepared and certain
as the dawn, and He will come to us as the [heavy] rain,
as the latter rain that waters the earth.
HOSEA 6:1, 3 AMPC

Each and every day, return to Me. Read My Word to understand Me. Recognize when My hand is shaping and molding your life. Look for Me in unexpected places—in the flowers that bloom, the snow that falls, the river that winds, and the breeze that caresses your cheek. See Me in the eye of a child, the kiss of a loved one, the scent on the air, the sun on your face, the flight of a bird, the joy in your heart.

I am in and all around you, keeping you safe, whispering in your ear, shielding you from danger, leading you through the labyrinth of life. You will find no better guide or teacher than Me and My Word. Learn us. Know us. Appreciate and cherish us. For we are one and the same. We are unstoppable. Like the streams that change the face of the earth over time, I am the living water that is helping you to carve out a godly life—for you and the children after you. As One who never changes, I will always come to you, certain as the dawn.

I see You, Lord Jesus. . .

To Serve with Love

"Now that I, your Lord and Teacher, have washed your feet, you also should wash one another's feet. I have set you an example that you should do as I have done for you. Very truly I tell you, no servant is greater than his master, nor is a messenger greater than the one who sent him. Now that you know these things, you will be blessed if you do them."
JOHN 13:14–17 NIV

Dear daughter, I ask you to follow the example of My Son. Serve others with love—whether they have asked you to or not. Will you do so? Do you do so? When Jesus was with the disciples, He got down on His knees to wash their feet. In so doing, He hoped they would see how they were to serve each other—no questions asked. And to allow others to serve them—no questions asked.

So do not protest when those you feel are "above" you seek to serve you. Allow them to experience the joy of a servant's heart. Do not try to pay them back, but allow them to feel the selfless love they have given you. Then go and do the same for some other soul. Without being asked, serve with love, compassion, desire, humility, and grace. Such an act on your knees will raise your spirit high—in this world and the next.

Lord, I will serve. . .

Rise Up!

My beloved spoke, and said to me: "Rise up, my love, my fair one, and come away. For lo, the winter is past, the rain is over and gone. The flowers appear on the earth; the time of singing has come, and the voice of the turtledove is heard in our land."
SONG OF SOLOMON 2:10–12 NKJV

Just when things look like they won't get any better, just when the cold and darkness seem to be swallowing you whole, remember Me. Come away with Me. Rise above the sorrows of this world. Like spring, I have come to warm your heart and lighten your load. In My presence, the winters of life hold no power—and the certainty of spring is on the rise. With Me, you can bloom where you are planted, no matter the earthly season. You will hear the voice of the birds who constantly live to sing praises in My name.

This is your season. This is your spring. This is your period of renewal, joy, warmth, and light. Let Me see your face, hear your voice. Know that when you are with Me, winter becomes a vague memory. So raise your arms and lift them up to the Son.

Lighten my load today, God. . .

Precious Lamb

"My sheep hear My voice, and I know them, and they follow Me. And I give them eternal life, and they shall never perish; neither shall anyone snatch them out of My hand. My Father, who has given them to Me, is greater than all; and no one is able to snatch them out of My Father's hand. I and My Father are one."
JOHN 10:27–30 NKJV

You are My precious lamb. There are so many things you have yet to discover, so many lessons you have yet to learn, so many paths you have yet to travel with Me. So follow closely. Spend much time in My presence. Then you will learn to know and recognize My voice when I speak. You will be familiar with My promptings, those sparks of divine intuition, inspiration, and ideas. There will be a wonderful connection between My spirit and yours. You will more easily be led to where I am guiding you.

Yes, learn My voice—every word, inflection, tone, and correction. Do not lose the import of what I say to you. Become so familiar with My way, My light, and My spark that you will be able to know Me, your Shepherd, in the flash of an eye and obey Me just as quickly, even when amid a crowded flock.

My Shepherd, lead me. . .

Perseverance

*It is profitable and fitting for you [now to complete the enterprise]
which more than a year ago you not only began, but were the
first to wish to do anything [about. . .]. So now finish doing it,
that your [enthusiastic] readiness in desiring it may be equalled
by your completion of it according to your ability and means.*

2 Corinthians 8:10–11 AMPC

You have come up against many obstacles in your efforts to complete an endeavor. You have suffered many trials. Come to Me for whatever extra energy and courage you need to finish the task at hand. Know that with My help, you can do anything. Know that I am working within you to help you bring things to completion. Never doubt for a second that this thing will be done.

You have the talent. You have the drive. You have the vision. You have the determination. You have the will. And I have given you the way. So do not despair but keep on keeping on. Persevere against all odds and you will be rewarded, for you have put feet to your faith. And that always makes Me smile, for it tends to make unbelievers gasp.

I come to You today, Father God. . .

Let Peace Reign

*And let the peace (soul harmony which comes) from
Christ rule (act as umpire continually) in your hearts
[deciding and settling with finality all questions that
arise in your minds, in that peaceful state] to which as
[members of Christ's] one body you were also called [to live].*
COLOSSIANS 3:15 AMPC

Your heart is thumping. Tears begin to well up in your eyes. To hide the fact that your fists are clenching and unclenching, you fold your arms in front of your chest. When your teeth begin to clamp together, you realize that this is not the time to make a decision. That's the Light from Me. That's My prompt, telling you to get while the getting is good. To extract yourself from the current situation. To come and seek My face.

If you allow Me, I will give you the peace you need before you speak. I will give you the wisdom you need to make the right decision, to help your heart and your mind come to the right conclusion. So, when your emotions threaten to take control, run—into My arms! Give Me your anger, your tears, your stress, your troubles. And I will help you give My peace the reins.

Wisdom-Giver, I seek Your face. . .

Resurrection Power

*God's Spirit is on me; he's chosen me to preach the Message
of good news to the poor, sent me to announce pardon to
prisoners and recovery of sight to the blind, to set the burdened
and battered free, to announce, "This is God's year to act!"*
LUKE 4:18–19 MSG

Do not worry about the power of temptation. Do not see the things that plague you as forces that cannot be overcome. Do not be concerned about the limited vision you have in certain areas of your life. Forget about all the issues, problems, and sometimes people that seem to weigh you down. I am here to help you. I can help break you out of any spiritual, emotional, financial, physical, and mental prison you are in. I have the healing power to restore your sight. I have the strength to carry whatever burdens you are bearing. I have the keenness of mind to deliver you from unhealthy relationships.

Simply come to Me, knowing that I, God, am going to change your life. I am going to raise you from whatever binds you. Trust in that resurrection power. . . . I am your example that anything is possible. Trust in Me.

Almighty God, I am tempted. . .

Uplifting Praise

*May the glory of the Lᴏʀᴅ endure forever; may the Lᴏʀᴅ
rejoice in His works. . . . I will sing to the Lᴏʀᴅ as long as I live;
I will sing praise to my God while I have my being. May my
meditation be sweet to Him; I will be glad in the Lᴏʀᴅ.*
Psᴀʟᴍ 104:31, 33–34 ɴᴋᴊᴠ

Lift your arms in praise, like a tree stretching to meet Me in the sky. Open your arms wide to capture the blessings of sunshine, rain, and snow. Raise your face, basking in the glow of My light, the power of My words, and the cleansing of My touch. Open your heart to the love I am ready to lavish upon you. Allow it to fill your entire being, leaving no corner untouched. Allow it to heal every disappointment, hurt, sorrow, and pain you have endured. Open up your soul to the truth I am waiting to set upon you. Allow it to expand your vision, until you see Me in every part of your life. Open up your spirit to hear My voice loud and clear. Allow it to change you from the inside out, making you more and more like Me. Lift your entire being up to Me. Be glad in all you are, in all that I have made you to be. Share the joy I bring to you, today and every day. Let not your heart ever be troubled. Let the sweetness of My name, My works, and My blessings overflow from My arms into yours.

Lord, I praise You. . .

The Ultimate Weapon

The weapons we fight with are not the weapons of the world.
On the contrary, they have divine power to demolish
strongholds. We demolish arguments and every pretension
that sets itself up against the knowledge of God, and we
take captive every thought to make it obedient to Christ.
2 CORINTHIANS 10:4–5 NIV

Thoughts are flitting through your mind all the time. They ricochet from one corner of your brain to another. Fortunately, you were not designed to follow every idea that comes into your head. If you did, you'd be going in a thousand different directions at once. That's because it's only the thoughts you *claim* that have the real power. And the more you own them, the longer you let them linger, the more powerful they get. Over time, these claimed thoughts grow feet, arms, and legs and take on a life of their own.

That is why you need to take all thoughts captive and bring them into My light. Test them against My Word. Realize that they are only thoughts, after all. Using My strength, My Word, you can regain control. The power you have in Me—that is your ultimate weapon. That is how you can change your thoughts, which will in turn change your mind, your life, and the world.

Truth-Teller, fill my mind with. . .

A Door Wide Open

For a wide door of opportunity for effectual
[service] has opened to me [there, a great and
promising one], and [there are] many adversaries.
1 CORINTHIANS 16:9 AMPC

I am calling you to a new space, a new area, a new opportunity, a new endeavor where you will do mighty things. Are your ears open? Do you hear My voice? Are you ready to glorify Me—or is something holding you back? Others initially refused their call. Moses didn't think he was a good enough speaker to talk for Me. Jonah initially refused to tackle the mission I had for him—so he became fish bait and was swallowed by a whale. Then there was Gideon, whom the angel of God addressed as a mighty warrior while he was still a farmer threshing grain.

Dare to believe that I am calling you. That although a new path may seem scary, it is the right path. That I will not send you out ill-equipped. Break free from the fetters of your comfortable world. Stop listening to the lies that you aren't good enough, smart enough, strong enough. You are a woman who, when she makes up her mind to, can accomplish anything with Me. I am holding the door wide open. Walk though to a new life.

Lord, I am listening. . .

Pouring Out

Hannah answered and said, "No, my lord, I am a woman of sorrowful spirit. I have drunk neither wine nor intoxicating drink, but have poured out my soul before the LORD. Do not consider your maidservant a wicked woman, for out of the abundance of my complaint and grief I have spoken until now."

1 SAMUEL 1:15–16 NKJV

Tell Me all that is on your mind. Hold nothing back! Pour your heart and soul out to Me. Let your armor drop. Let your guard down. Allow nothing to stand between us—no weapon, no shield, no shame. Enough of the brave front, the facade, the mask that you wear in front of so many others. Show Me the true you. I will not turn you away. I will not mock you. Instead, I want to know you. I crave to know exactly what is going on in your life.

There is no need for you to sugarcoat anything. Believe Me— I have seen it all, so nothing you say is going to shock Me. Let's talk together. Let's get it all down to the bare bones so we can build your life up again. There is no need to fear Me. Simply come. Talk. And pour out your soul. I am here to receive all that you say, all that you are, all that you have been—and help fill you up again.

I lay it all before You, Lord Jesus. . .

Remember Lot's Wife

*And when they had brought them forth, they said,
Escape for your life! Do not look behind you or stop
anywhere in the whole valley; escape to the mountains
[of Moab], lest you be consumed. . . . But [Lot's] wife
looked back from behind him, and she became a pillar of salt.*
GENESIS 19:17, 26 AMPC

How willing are you to follow Me? What are you willing to leave behind on the material plane to become closer to Me on the spiritual plane? How much are you willing to sacrifice so you can truly move forward?

Each and every day you have a choice to make—to come with Me down the path I have laid out for you or to stay where you are, no matter the consequences. It's all up to you. If you disregard My pleas and stay on the plane of your current existence, you may just end up stuck there, wondering where your opportunity went. But if you decide to listen to Me, to follow My lead, you will find yourself going forward to the mountain, continually rising up higher and higher, closer and closer to Me and the kingdom of heaven.

Perhaps you may start out with Me but then, longing for what had been, look back at what you've left behind. Chances are, that constant looking back will bring not only discontentment but more trouble in the long run. So, decide. What are you going to do—walk with Me, eyes looking forward, or look back at your own peril?

I will walk with You, God. . .

Eagles' Wings

*"You have seen what I did to Egypt and how I carried
you on eagles' wings and brought you to me. If you
will listen obediently to what I say and keep my covenant,
out of all peoples you'll be my special treasure."*
EXODUS 19:4–5 MSG

I have seen what you've been up to. I have you constantly in My sights. In fact, I travel to and fro over the face of the earth to keep an eye on all My people. My message to you today is to not despair. There will be times when your plans go awry. When you come against too many obstacles. When you come to a fork in the road and are just not sure of which path to take. All of this is part of the journey. All of this is what keeps drawing you back to Me. All of this is what will make you stronger so you can sense My presence, look for My hand, and seek My voice.

You are My special girl. You are My extraordinary possession. I have been, am, and remain only a sigh away. Call Me. Speak to Me. Ask Me whatever you will. I am here for you. As in times past, I will carry you on eagles' wings and bring you back to Me. So go. Obey. Love. And above all, do not despair. I am here to swoop you up at any point in time.

Father God, I'm thankful to have You with me on the journey. . .

The Promises Foretold

*As it is written, I have made you the father of many nations.
[He was appointed our father] in the sight of God in
Whom he believed, Who gives life to the dead and
speaks of the nonexistent things that [He has foretold
and promised] as if they [already] existed.*

ROMANS 4:17 AMPC

You are a mighty woman. You are an amazing creature, built to accomplish amazing things. You are brave, determined, loving, kind, gentle, joyful, patient, promising, awesome, faithful, humble, worthy of sacrifice, and more! "But," you may say, "these things are not true of me. They are things that I want to be, that I strive for. But I am so far away from being the creature You want me to be—and now say that I already am!" Yet that's just what faith is.

I am telling you things that, in My eyes, already exist. That is how I see you—as a woman, complete in every way, shape, and form. I am not restricted or limited by time. I can see who you are about to become. So keep the faith. Understand the promises. You have a God who can grow a life inside a ninety-year-old woman! Do not place limits on a God who will not and cannot be chained down! What I have promised you has, in My eyes, already come through. So, daughter, simply have faith! And all that is written about your new life in Christ will be—or actually, already is!

Help me keep faith, heavenly Father. . .

No Problem Too Small

"Are not two sparrows sold for a penny? Yet not one of them will fall to the ground outside your Father's care. And even the very hairs of your head are all numbered. So don't be afraid; you are worth more than many sparrows."
MATTHEW 10:29–31 NIV

I am interested in every detail of your life. There is no problem too small, no discouragement too vague, no grievance so slight that I am not concerned about it. I have told you before how important you are to Me. So when you come to Me, do not hide anything. Do not let the slightest problem furrow your brow. Let it all out. When you do, your heart will feel lighter. Your creases will ease. Your anger will dissipate, your sorrow will turn to joy, your worries will be sent packing, your disappointments will fade away, your shame will lessen, and your frustrations will be eased. What once frightened you will diminish when put into words, brought into My light, and left at the foot of My cross. All this weight that you carry will slough off of your shoulders and onto Mine. So come. Bring Me your all. Drop it at My feet. And when you are ready, leave My presence as light, airy, and free as a little sparrow.

Lighten my spirit, Almighty Father. . .

Continuous Spring

Whoever takes a drink of the water that I will give him shall never, no never, be thirsty any more. But the water that I will give him shall become a spring of water welling up (flowing, bubbling) [continually] within him unto (into, for) eternal life.
JOHN 4:14 AMPC

I am your living water. When you trust and believe in Me, when you rely on Me like no other, when you take a drink of the water I can give you, your entire life will change. My water will begin a work like no other. It will give you inner strength and courage, inner wisdom and clarity. You will be overflowing with an abundant supply of everything you need to face the outer world. People will come to you to be refreshed, for you are not a stagnant being but an ever-flowing river of hope, love, faith, and charity.

All that you need, I am. All that you can be, I can sustain. All that you desire will be met and satisfied by My ever-flowing, ever-abundant living water. You need not strain any longer but simply believe, trust, and rely on the Word that I have spoken, the Word that changes lives forevermore, the Word that gives you an endless supply of love and water for life, to forever change your inner and therefore the outer world.

Living Water, I thirst for You. . .

Childlike Wonder

And overwhelming astonishment and ecstasy seized them all,
and they recognized and praised and thanked God; and
they were filled with and controlled by reverential fear
and kept saying, We have seen wonderful and strange
and incredible and unthinkable things today!

LUKE 5:26 AMPC

After spending time in My presence, go out with a sense of wonder. Know that I can do amazing and powerful things, things you can't even imagine. I have ideas for your life that you could never think possible—but I am the Lord of impossibilities. Look for Me to amaze you. Expect the unexpected blessings.

Look for Me around every corner, and you will find Me. Maintain that mind-set, that joy of expectancy all day. Recognize Me moving in your life. Praise and thank Me for every blessing bestowed upon you. I am the Lord of miracles. I am the Lord who can give you unsurpassed peace. I can raise people from the dead, heal the lame, turn water into wine, calm the sea, and still the wind. With a wave of My hand, a nod of My head. . .the world is forever changed. Live with a childlike wonder, curious as to what I will do next. In doing so, you will be living a joy-filled life.

Miracle-Giver, You fill me with wonder. . .

_____

_____

_____

_____

_____

_____

_____

_____

_____

_____

_____

_____

_____

_____

_____

_____

_____

_____

_____

Heart Prayers

"Before I had finished praying in my heart, I saw Rebekah coming out with her water jug on her shoulder. She went down to the spring and drew water."

GENESIS 24:45 NLT

I know exactly what you need and when you need it. I know the thoughts of all people, including you and those around you. For me, there are no surprises. Before you are even done praying, before the words have left your lips, an answer is on its way. There can be no delay. Know this as a fact. Live this in your life. Be assured that there is not one thing I do not know. Understand that all My knowledge is too much for you. And that there is a reason you don't know or have all the answers. That's what this faith thing is all about.

To be saved from the world of humankind and your own self, you must have complete faith and trust that I am here. I know all. I am listening to your prayers. I am always moving and putting things in place for your good. I am always working in your life because your life is precious to Me. And nothing on heaven or earth can separate you from My love. So come. Pray. And I will move in your life for good.

Nothing can separate me from Your love, Lord. . .

Mighty Warrior

One day the angel of God came and sat down under the oak in Ophrah that belonged to Joash the Abiezrite, whose son Gideon was threshing wheat in the winepress. . . . The angel of God appeared to him and said, "God is with you, O mighty warrior!"
JUDGES 6:11–12 MSG

I see things in you that you have no idea you possess. I see you as brave, determined, loving, kind, gentle, and simply amazing. You see, I know what you are equipped for. Every moment, hour, day, month, year, you are becoming more and more of what I created you to be. You may be saying to yourself, "Why I'm no one special. Just an ordinary career woman, mother, wife, daughter, sister, friend, artist, or believer." But woman, you are so much more. You are mighty in courage and love. You have untold power that I have given you, beyond what you could ever dream of. There is so much more to you than meets the eye—and most of it lies within. I am here to awaken your courage. To draw you unto Me. To convince you that you can do whatever you set your mind to. To know that the strength you already have is what you are going to draw on wherever I send you.

When you are living in My power, when you are allowing Me to work through you, when you take Me with you every step of the way, you are not just any woman. You are a mighty warrior.

Heavenly Creator, thank You for seeing me. . .

Milk and Honey

*"If the L*ᴏʀᴅ *delights in us, then He will bring us into this land and give it to us, 'a land which flows with milk and honey.' Only do not rebel against the L*ᴏʀᴅ*, nor fear the people of the land, for they are our bread; their protection has departed from them, and the L*ᴏʀᴅ *is with us. Do not fear them."*
Nᴜᴍʙᴇʀs 14:8–9 ɴᴋᴊᴠ

You need not be afraid of anything. No matter what you face, I will fight for you. There is no foe who can withstand My power. There is no giant I cannot slay. So why fear the monsters built up in your imagination? Why talk yourself out of getting in the water without even wading in up to your ankles?

Woman, you are more than flesh and blood. You are spirit—and when you abide in Me, I am abiding in you. There is no foe we cannot face together. So do not lose courage just when you are on the edge of entering the Promised Land. For if you do, you may spend more time in the wilderness than you want to. Instead, delight in Me. Seek My face, courage, heart for battle. I will give you everything you need to vanquish every fear and foe—imaginary or not. Do not shrink back to the old land, where you were enslaved by temptation, fear, and angst. Stop murmuring. Pick up your spiritual armor and go forward with My name on your lips, My power in your soul, and the Holy Spirit's strength to conquer all. This land is yours.

Father God, I delight in You...

The Name Jesus

"Let it be known to you all, and to all the people of Israel, that by the name of Jesus Christ of Nazareth, whom you crucified, whom God raised from the dead, by Him this man stands here before you whole."

ACTS 4:10 NKJV

The power of My name—*Jesus*. There is no other name with such authority. To those who are walking in darkness, *Jesus* brings light. To those who are groping the walls as if they were blind, *Jesus* provides direction, a new road, a new life. To those who are trembling, *Jesus* brings strength. To those who are weak kneed, *Jesus* brings courage. To those who are unprotected and unsheltered, *Jesus* provides a shield and a home. To those who are ill of body, mind, spirit, and soul, *Jesus* heals. And the key to unleashing all this power to the individual is faith—faith that I am the Light that will lead you out of darkness. That I am the One who can give you a new vision. That I am the One who can strengthen, protect, shield, and heal. Yes, I am the One with the power, but you are the one who must have the belief to apply that power to your life and see it live in every aspect of your being. It is only My power combined with your belief in Me and My name that will make you whole.

There is power in Your name, Lord Jesus. . .

Touching the Untouchable

Jesus reached out and touched him. "I am willing," he said.
"Be healed!" And instantly the leprosy disappeared.
MATTHEW 8:3 NLT

Never hesitate to approach Me. Never think that your sins are so great that you cannot face Me. Never believe that I am too busy to tend to you, that you could ever be a bother. Never imagine that your faith is so little that I cannot use you. Allow nothing to hinder your coming.

Remember the leper who approached Me? In that day, he was considered an "untouchable." Yet he broke through the crowds. He humbled himself before Me. He worshipped Me, no holds barred, and then demonstrated his faith by saying, "Lord, if You want to, You can not only heal me but make me clean." What courage! What belief! Of course I was willing! I then touched the untouchable leper—and healed him. *Instantly*, he was cured *and* cleansed! Do you need curing? Do you need cleansing? Do you have courage? Come to Me. Do not hesitate. Do not let other seekers crowd you out. Do not let mockers steer you away. Do not let your state of mind, body, or spirit trip you up. Come. No matter how untouchable you feel, I will touch your life and make you whole once more.

Use me, Father God. . .

_____

_____

_____

_____

_____

_____

_____

_____

_____

_____

_____

_____

_____

_____

_____

_____

_____

_____

_____

_____

_____

_____

_____

_____

Soft Hearts

*O come, let us worship and bow down, let us kneel before
the Lord our Maker [in reverent praise and supplication].
For He is our God and we are the people of His pasture
and the sheep of His hand. Today, if you will hear
His voice, harden not your hearts.*
PSALM 95:6–8 AMPC

I hold this day in My hands—in trust for you. Make of it what you will. Look for opportunities behind each and every door. Seek to love each life you come into contact with. Look with curiosity at what may be revealed. Be gentle with yourself and those around you. And with all joy, tackle each task before you, knowing that all you receive is from My hand. Listen for My voice, seek My path, walk My way and you will never find yourself alone, frightened, or out of My will.

Keep your heart soft, pliable, malleable, open to My suggestion, My leading. Step in time with your spirit, allowing it free rein as it links up with Mine. There is nothing more beautiful in this world than a woman of God quietly obeying My commands and finding contentment in loving and serving others. Stay close, woman. I have need of you today.

Master Potter, mold me today. . .

Making Room

*We can make our plans, but the L*ord *determines our steps.*
P*roverbs* 16:9 nlt

You are so eager to know what tomorrow may bring. You are so attached to plans of your own making, for women rarely want to be surprised. But I am asking you to detach from the outcome of your life, to be okay with *not* knowing the end of the story. Instead, have faith that I am leading you in the right direction. You may have a general idea of how you'd like your life to come out, but I am the One who will take you step by step to reach the dream I have had in mind for you from the beginning.

So trust Me. Know that all I want is for your good—and the good of those whose lives you will touch. Just take My hand. Be confident that I will not lead you astray but place you exactly where you were meant to be. In fact, that's where you are today— just where I want you to be. So relax. Live with joy in the moment, in the now. Continue to make your plans but leave room for Me to move in your journey. For only with Me will you reach places you would never dream of. For only with Me will you have the courage, the fortitude, and the perseverance to become all you were made to be.

With You, heavenly Father, I can. . .

Soul Guard

Now to Him who is able to keep you from stumbling, and to present you faultless before the presence of His glory with exceeding joy, to God our Savior, who alone is wise, be glory and majesty, dominion and power, both now and forever. Amen.

JUDE 1:24–25 NKJV

I am beside you—not to watch you stumble, but to catch you when you lose your balance. Not to see how far you can go without My help, but to strengthen you every step of the Way. Consider Me your Soul Guard, King, and Servant all rolled into one. I see you as the perfect creation. With Me, you cannot fail. Beside Me, you are undefeatable. Behind Me you are sheltered. Below Me, you are on solid ground.

I am the All-Powerful who strengthens you, the All-Present who never leaves you alone, the All-Knowing who answers every question you could ever imagine—and ones you have yet to think of. So do not worry about tripping over a stone. I can lift you above any impediments you could ever imagine. Together, we will win the race of glory, victory, and love—here on earth and in heaven!

Almighty God, I will not fail because. . .

_____

_____

_____

_____

_____

_____

_____

_____

_____

_____

_____

_____

_____

_____

_____

_____

_____

_____

_____

_____

Power in Numbers

God's Word is an indispensable weapon. In the same way, prayer is essential in this ongoing warfare. Pray hard and long. Pray for your brothers and sisters. Keep your eyes open. Keep each other's spirits up so that no one falls behind or drops out.
EPHESIANS 6:17–18 MSG

You have been put in a family of God for a reason: there is power in numbers, for whenever and wherever two or three believers are together, I AM there in the midst of them. And that is some astounding power that becomes even more potent and amazing when you gather to pray the Word, the scripture. So when you are in the midst of a great battle, do not shrink back. Instead, move forward with another believer. Take the Word and give it life by speaking it aloud. Agree on the truth of the scripture. And pray, pray, pray. Pray for salvation of unbelievers. Pray for the needs of your brothers and sisters in Christ. Pray for your family; the world; the persecuted; the maligned; the politicians; the rulers of nations; the imprisoned; the church; the ill of body, mind, and spirit. Look at the world's woes and bring them to Me. When you do so, I will be moved into action. Meanwhile, I await your word, your movement, your exercising of faith.

Lord, I gather with other believers. . .

Dream-Provider

Do nothing from factional motives [through contentiousness, strife, selfishness, or for unworthy ends] or prompted by conceit and empty arrogance. Instead, in the true spirit of humility (lowliness of mind) let each regard the others as better than and superior to himself [thinking more highly of one another than you do of yourselves]. Let each of you esteem and look upon and be concerned for not [merely] his own interests, but also each for the interests of others.

PHILIPPIANS 2:3–4 AMPC

Take each day's events as work you can do for Me. Never see anything as an interruption but as a potential new assignment. Allow My power to flow through you so that you will have the strength and wisdom to meet all challenges. The only block in the channel may be yourself. Clear the way so that I can flow directly through you with no hindrance, such as fear, loathing, greed, pettiness, unforgiveness, malice, etc. Do not be so focused on yourself and your *own* dreams, needs, and desires that you miss an opportunity to be the dream-provider for someone else. This selflessness is the mark of a true woman of the Way. Work to joyfully move others ahead of yourself, and in so doing, you will find yourself even more blessed.

All-Powerful God, I am working for You. . .

I Am

If you do not believe that I am He [Whom I claim to be—
if you do not adhere to, trust in, and rely on Me], you will
die in your sins. Then they said to Him, Who are You anyway?
Jesus replied, [Why do I even speak to you!] I am exactly
what I have been telling you from the first.
JOHN 8:24–25 AMPC

I am the One who brings you light each morning. I am the cool glass of Living Water on a hot, dry day. I am the beacon that guides you home from foreign shores. I am the power you use when you want to move mountains. I am the invisible wind that makes the leaves dance in midair. I am the love you see in a child's eyes. I am the words of love whispered by the man of your dreams. I am the riches you never imagined gaining at the end of the rainbow. I am the deep sigh that refreshes your weary bones. I am the peace that comes with the embrace of a well-loved and loving friend. I am the Father who always has your welfare first and foremost in his mind. I am the bloom of beauty upon your favorite rose. I am the boat that carries you from one destination to another. I am the love that transcends all languages. I am the One you can trust above all others. You need not scramble to find Me, for I am always with you. I am the answer you have always sought. I am all things to you—and you are everything to Me.

Father, my heart is thankful. . .

Rejoice in Today!

Today is a new day—made by Me, just for you! Receive it with joy—for that is how it has been given. No matter what the day brings, sing praises that you are here to live it! You have taken the good path, the narrow way. But it is the joyous path, all the same. For you have found Me. And I am rejoicing in you!

Here with Me in this wonderful world you will be well-fed, rested, watched over, and loved. So, rejoice! Laugh! Love! There is no greater moment than this present one. There is no greater day than today. Do not fret about the future. Do not mourn the events of the past. Instead, find joy in the now. Find joy in your loved ones. Find joy in the job. Today has been made by Me and put into your hands. So make it a good day. Bless everyone you come into contact with—friend or foe! There is no greater way to spend the day than in love, love, love. And that is something worth celebrating!

My Loving Provider, today I celebrate. . .

_____
_____
_____
_____
_____
_____
_____
_____
_____
_____
_____
_____
_____
_____
_____
_____
_____
_____
_____
_____
_____
_____

Blanketed with Love

The Lord your God is in the midst of you, a Mighty One,
a Savior [Who saves]! He will rejoice over you with joy;
He will rest [in silent satisfaction] and in His love He will
be silent and make no mention [of past sins, or even
recall them]; He will exult over you with singing.

ZEPHANIAH 3:17 AMPC

In these precious moments, allow Me to blanket you with My love. Rest in Me as I cover you from heel to head. Let My warmth nourish your bosom. Allow My light to remove all chill and darkness. Let My wisdom clear all the cobwebs in your mind. I, your warrior, have fought for you. I cannot help but sing about you—day and night, for you delight Me! Even though you have sinned and may continue to sin, I will not mention your misdeeds once you have asked for forgiveness. They will have disappeared, as if they never existed. For I know that in your heart is love for Me. And that love makes the light I give you shine even brighter. So rest here in My presence. Take this time to be refueled. There is no rush. There is no worry. You are exactly where you need to be—with Me at this time. On this earth.

Giver of Rest, today I will pause. . .

Burden Bearer

*"I took the world off your shoulders, freed you from a life
of hard labor. You called to me in your pain; I got you out
of a bad place. I answered you from where the thunder
hides, I proved you at Meribah Fountain."*

PSALM 81:6–7 MSG

My Son, Jesus, came down to earth and lived among you. He took all your burdens upon Himself. He freed you who were captive to the missteps that plagued you and kept you from doing all that I had planned for you since the beginning of time.

You cried out for Me, and so I rescued you, brought you to a better place. I spoke to you from the mountains, showed you how to live, and where to go when you needed to get closer to Me. I left the Holy Spirit with you, a personal guide to the most wonderful life you can live in the light.

But you refuse to remember. You continue to live as if all these things have not been done for you. You act as if the burdens in your life are ones you can actually bear. They are not! Come! Now! Bring all your cares and woes, your doubts and frustrations, your anxieties and fears to Me! Lay them down at My feet. Only *I* can pick up and bear such a load!

Then rise up anew. Breathe, live, love, and be who you were created to be. A follower in and of Christ!

I lay my worries at Your feet, Father God. . .

....
....
....
....
....
....
....
....
....
....
....
....
....
....
....
....
....
....
....
....
....
....
....

Crossroads

I [the Lord] will instruct you and teach you in the way you should go; I will counsel you with My eye upon you. Be not like the horse or the mule, which lack understanding, which must have their mouths held firm with bit and bridle, or else they will not come with you.
PSALM 32:8–9 AMPC

Each day you may find yourself at a crossroads, wondering which path to take. Sometimes your choice may seem like a small, almost insignificant decision. But in your walk with Me, every step you take counts. Every choice has its consequence.

Yet do not be anxious. Do not fret. Simply spend time in My Word and in My company. I, your teacher, will instruct you. Then you will learn who I am and know what I would have you do in each and every situation. But if at any time you are uncertain, pause at the crossroads. Ask Me which way you should go. Then, only when you clearly hear My voice, choose your path and step out in faith. Do not be slow. Do not have the stubbornness of a mule. But take courage, be bold, filled with the assurance that I have already gone ahead and paved the way.

If you do not hear My voice, wait upon Me. Know there is a reason your feet are stayed. I have My eye upon you. And I will not lead you into evil, only good. Rest in that knowledge.

Give me guidance today, Lord Jesus. . .

Praise the Lord

Let all that I am praise the LORD; may I never forget the good things he does for me. He forgives all my sins and heals all my diseases. . . . He has removed our sins as far from us as the east is from the west.

PSALM 103:2–3, 12 NLT

Are you still holding on to how you missed the mark (sinned) a day, week, month, year, decade ago? My child, do not do this to yourself! Do not continually muse over your misdeeds; mutter over how you continue to make the same mistake; or, even worse, alienate yourself from Me because you don't feel worthy to be in My presence.

Stop in this moment. Know that I have already forgiven you. For My eye is constantly upon you, examining your heart, looking to see how you are, concerned for your being, like a mother who looks out for her precious child. I know you will make mistakes. And My plan has already allowed for them. Thus, understand and know that I no longer see your sins. In fact, I have removed them from you. So think of them no more, for to do so diffuses My strength and power within you. And I have many things for you to do in My name.

Mistake-Eraser, I thank You. . .

Be Confident

Delight yourself also in the Lord, and He will give you the desires and secret petitions of your heart. Commit your way to the Lord [roll and repose each care of your load on Him]; trust (lean on, rely on, and be confident) also in Him and He will bring it to pass.
PSALM 37:4–5 AMPC

I do not want to be a part of your daily drudge, like a meeting you have to attend. I want you to run to Me, to want to be with Me, like a child longing to be in her mother's presence, bursting with joy as she scrambles up onto her lap, leans back against her breast, and finds a peace and joy like no other.

Come to Me like that little child. Delight in My company. Tell Me your plans, your dreams. Leave with Me all your worries and what-ifs. I will take care of them in good order. Then trust Me to bring your desires to pass in the way that best serves you and My grand plan. For as you love Me more and more, slowly My desires are what you grow to desire.

Remember to rely on Me more than yourself and those around you. Trust in Me more than you do the temporal things and beings in your world. Remember that I have so many more allies at My disposal, angels who run to do My bidding. Be confident in all this.

Heavenly Father, I trust You will take care of. . .

All Ways, All Days

But I will sing of Your mighty strength and power; yes, I will sing aloud of Your mercy and loving-kindness in the morning; for You have been to me a defense (a fortress and a high tower) and a refuge in the day of my distress.

PSALM 59:16 AMPC

Yes, sing, sing, sing of My strength and power. Shout about My mercy, forgiveness, and overflowing love for you. And watch walls as thick as Jericho tumble down, because your faith united with My power can destroy any barriers you come up against.

Know that I am what stands between you and the things that would harm you. When you come to Me, when you realize My presence, you are assured of My protection. It is only when you lose that awareness of Me that you begin to fear and fret.

But as soon as you begin to turn toward Me, to trust Me, to reach out your hand and put it in My own, you find a strength that is not your own; a confidence that is otherworldly; an infusion of love that is overwhelming; and a peace of mind, heart, body, soul, and spirit that is unimaginable.

So sing. Praise. Reach out your hand. Feel My power entering you. And know that I stand with you in all ways, all days.

I claim the promise of Your protection, Lord Jesus. . .

From Discord to Delight

"I take joy in doing your will, my God,
for your instructions are written on my heart."
PSALM 40:8 NLT

Feeling unsettled? Pause in your daily doings and get away by yourself, even if only for a few moments. Prayerfully look within. See where you may be walking out of step with the Holy Spirit I have left for you. He is your gift, to help you find your way.

When you are not following the Spirit's promptings, when you are not heeding His whispers of *"Pssst. This way! Come this way!"* you will feel the otherworldly discord in every area of your life, leading to confusion, and the confusion to anxiety.

Have the promptings you received not made sense to you with your limited thinking? Were you not exactly sure whose voice you were hearing? Whatever the case, have no fear. Call Me and I will come near. I will sidle up beside you and help you find your footing again. I will help you hone in on the true voice so that you can get out of your current wilderness and find your way back to your Promised Land. I am your compass and your guide, always pointing you in the right direction so that there is harmony in your life. So that you will no longer feel the discord but only the joy in doing the will of your Lord.

Come away with Me. Let's consider. Let's move from discord to delight.

I call on Your name, Father. . .

Relief from Unbelief

*When doubts filled my mind, your comfort gave me
renewed hope and cheer. . . . The LORD is my fortress;
my God is the mighty rock where I hide.*
PSALM 94:19, 22 NLT

Why oh why are you so riddled with doubts about Me, My power, My strength, My love, My ability, My longing to help you, and even at times My very existence? Even worse, why do you hide those doubts from Me?

Have you not heard the story of the man whose boy needed healing? The one who asked Me to take pity on him and his son and pleaded, "If there's anything you can do, please help us"?

My reply was and still is to all doubters: anything and everything is possible for the one who believes—in Me, My power, My strength, My longing to help you, My love, My ability.

So come to Me now, My beloved, with all your doubts and fears. Spill them out. Spell them out. Then ask Me to help you increase your belief in Me, to teach you how to overcome any stumbling blocks in your faith. For in doing so, you will immediately find relief for your suffering. You will sense My Spirit. You will have a new sense of hope and cheer as I take you by the hand and lift you to your feet.

I sense Your Spirit, Lord. . .

_____
_____
_____
_____
_____
_____
_____
_____
_____
_____
_____
_____
_____
_____
_____
_____
_____
_____
_____
_____
_____
_____
_____
_____
_____
_____
_____

Divine Interruptions

The LORD gave this message to Jonah son of Amittai: "Get up and go to the great city of Nineveh. . . ." But Jonah got up and went in the opposite direction to get away from the LORD. . . . But the LORD hurled a powerful wind over the sea, causing a violent storm that threatened to break the ship apart.

JONAH 1:1–4 NLT

You may feel as if your days are filled with interruptions, things, and events that are keeping you from living your "real" life. Take heart. Relax. Because those interruptions *are* your real life.

Jonah must have felt frustrated when I told him to ignore his "real" life and go to Nineveh. So he went the other way, determined to do what he wanted to do—and ended up suffering, as did those around him, for ignoring the divine interruption. In the end, he wound up in Nineveh anyway, just as I had planned.

And that's the point. Your life is My plan—not your own. There are lessons you are meant to learn. So do not allow frustration to take hold when you find your life interrupted. Do not disobey when I speak a new plan into your life. Instead, be vigilant in seeking My face, obeying My directive, and keeping yourself and your life in line with My plan. In doing so, I know how many storms you will avoid.

Awaken me to Your divine interruptions, Father. . .

Finding Life

*Whoever goes hunting for what is right
and kind finds life itself—glorious life!*
PROVERBS 21:21 MSG

I am interested in your life. Every tear, every smile, every joy, every heartache. I am looking to connect with you in everything you experience—every sunset you see, rainbow you chase, and storm cloud you fear. As you seek Me, I seek you. To chat. To walk. To dream.

So seek Me as ardently as I seek you. For I am always near, just waiting for you to respond to My knock, to open the door and eat with Me. It is then you will find and uncover the life you were born, made, meant to live. It is then you will find the way, the truth, and the life.

When you search for, find, and recover Me, when you bring Me into your life, you will be unable to contain your joy. You, like David, will break forth in dancing, singing, and praising Me with all your might. You will be celebrating My kingdom.

Today, I earnestly seek You, Father God. . .

Bask in the Son-Shine

"Look at the lilies and how they grow. They don't work or make their clothing, yet Solomon in all his glory was not dressed as beautifully as they are. And if God cares so wonderfully for flowers that are here today and thrown into the fire tomorrow, he will certainly care for you. Why do you have so little faith?"
Luke 12:27–28 NLT

Stress and strain are for nonbelievers, not you. You are to be like the lily. Consider that flower. How it grows up into what it has already been designed to be. There is no struggle, no stress, no strain. It neither toils nor spins. Instead it just basks in the sunshine, drinks in the water, feeds off the soil, and takes in the air. So should it be with you.

Do not struggle. Simply allow yourself to grow up into what you have been created to be—My child. Consider how you do not need to work at this. Simply bask in the Son-shine. Drink in the living water. Feed off and be grounded in the soil of the Word. And take in the counsel of the Holy Spirit.

Trust Me in all this and you will find your life blessed, your growth unbounded, and your leaves green, bearing fruit regardless of the weather—inside and out.

Lord Jesus, I am blessed beyond measure. . .

I Am There

My help comes from the LORD, who made heaven and earth!
He will not let you stumble; the one who watches over you
will not slumber. Indeed, he who watches over Israel never
slumbers or sleeps. The LORD himself watches over you!
The LORD stands beside you as your protective shade.
PSALM 121:2–5 NLT

I never sleep. No matter when you seek Me, you will find Me, waiting, watching. No matter where you are, I am with you. When you call Me, it's not so much that I have not been with you, but that, because you have called, you have become more aware of My existence.

Remember, I have said that I will never leave you nor forsake you. Live in the truth of that promise, that knowledge. You can neither outlive, outrun, or outpace Me. For I am everywhere, in all things. It is in Me that you move, live, and have your very being.

So if you wake up in the middle of the night, speak to Me. I am there, longing to commune with you. If you are far away from home, never fear. I am where you are. If you have drifted away from My Spirit, afraid I will not recognize your voice, speak anyway, for I am listening. And I will answer. Nothing can separate Me or My love from you. Rest in this. Let it give you peace.

Heavenly Father, I know You are never far from me. . .

Worth Your While

Then the LORD said to Moses, "Look, I have specifically chosen Bezalel son of Uri, grandson of Hur, of the tribe of Judah. I have filled him with the Spirit of God, giving him great wisdom, ability, and expertise in all kinds of crafts. He is a master craftsman."
EXODUS 31:1–4 NLT

You have been given a special talent, an ability, a gift. Use it for My glory.

I have filled you with My Spirit, with My wisdom to do what no one else can do. And all in accordance with My plan and purpose. This talent comes with a passion. For it you need persistence. So look to Me. I will help you to keep on keeping on.

Do not allow others to dissuade you from plying your gift. Find a way to feed the passion for the craft that only your hands can undertake. Do not let your hands lie limp. But take up the task, keep at it, practice. And as you do so, you will improve. It will become worth your while. And sooner or later, it will reach the right hearts, find its own path, take on a life of its own.

Whatever you do, do not let circumstances dictate the work of your hands. Find a way to use what you've been given, to do what you've been appointed to do, in whatever way possible, be it little or small. And I will be glorified.

I will use the gifts I've been given, Lord. . .

Be Still

The Lord of hosts is with us; the God of Jacob is our Refuge (our Fortress and High Tower). Selah [pause, and calmly think of that]! . . . Let be and be still, and know (recognize and understand) that I am God.
PSALM 46:7, 10 AMPC

It is in the stillness that you hear, that you know, that you feel who I truly am.

So be still. Allow your hands to sit quietly in your lap. Relax your jaw, neck, shoulders, back—every part of your being, from the top of your hairs, which I have counted, to the tips of your toes, which I have formed, molded, and shaped.

Allow your breath to become slow and steady, a reminder of the undulating waves that softly break upon the shore and then drift back to the sea. Become aware of the rhythm, the cycle that all creation dances to.

Now that your body is still, turn your thoughts to Me. Sink into Me. Lean back against Me and feel My chest move up and down with each breath. Be filled with the light of My presence as we sit together, you and I, in the stillness of time, space, and spirit.

Yes, I am with you. You are secure in My arms. So rest easy. Know, recognize, understand that I am the very air you breathe and all that you need. Be still. And know.

You are my Refuge, Lord Jesus. . .

Goodness in the Land of the Living

[What, what would have become of me] had I not believed that I would see the Lord's goodness in the land of the living! Wait and hope for and expect the Lord; be brave and of good courage and let your heart be stout and enduring. Yes, wait for and hope for and expect the Lord.
PSALM 27:13–14 AMPC

I am doing something in your life, something that you cannot yet see. Know that all will be well. All is meant for good.

Do not despair. For in doing so, you distance yourself from Me. Instead, pray. There is supernatural power there. Have faith that all will be well. That you will see My goodness in your life.

Wait. Hope. Expect. Keep up your courage. Be patient. Have confidence. Trust that I am working, no matter how difficult things may seem. Remember that I see far beyond time and space. I know what lies ahead for you. And it is all for good. There is nothing to fear. No reason to fret. A new beginning lies before you. Beyond this point are things you never imagined or dreamed, things to give you hope, joy, and song. For now, hang on to My Word. Know the answers are there, awaiting your prayer. Abide in My light and presence. And I will strengthen you with My divine and eternal companionship.

Although I don't always recognize Your hand at work, God. . .

The Power of Harmony

*"The person who trusts me will not only do what I'm doing
but even greater things, because I, on my way to the Father,
am giving you the same work to do that I've been doing.
You can count on it. From now on, whatever you request along
the lines of who I am and what I am doing, I'll do it. That's
how the Father will be seen for who he is in the Son.
I mean it. Whatever you request in this way, I'll do."*
JOHN 14:12–14 MSG

Line up with My will and watch our combined power erupt into miracles!

Do not be like Jacob, who wrestled with My will for his life. I do not want you limping around but walking tall. When you are aligned with Me, you will be a power to be reckoned with! For you will be in total harmony with Me—just as humankind was supposed to be from the very beginning, from the creation of the world.

I sent My Son to earth to be your example, to save you from yourself, to reunite you with Me, to give you My vision for your life. So do not cloud your eyes with thoughts and desires that are not of Me. Instead, set your sights on the tasks I have set before you, the continuation of the work I began—loving, caring, praying, communing with, and seeking Me. Then I will do what you have asked.

Almighty Father, reveal Your will. . .

Ask. Reach. Open.

We are not set right with God by rule-keeping but only through personal faith in Jesus Christ. . . . Convinced that no human being can please God by self-improvement, we believed in Jesus as the Messiah so that we might be set right before God by trusting in the Messiah, not by trying to be good.

GALATIANS 2:16 MSG

Rules, rules, rules. They will not save you. In fact, they will only stress you out even more. For there is no way you will be able to obey them all, keep them all, follow them all to perfection.

I am not asking for you to be perfect in every way. I am simply asking you to believe in Me. To have complete faith in Me. To trust that I truly am the Way, the Life, and the Truth. To follow in My footsteps, the path I have laid out before you. That is the only way you and your ways and life will be made right with Me.

Do you understand? If not, pray for such understanding. Make your seeking out and following Me the most important thing in your life. Speak to Me often, asking Me every little thing. I thrill at the sound of your voice. I long for the touch of your hand. I ache to share My life and light with you. So ask. Reach. Open. I am here, waiting to hear, connect, and fill.

I am reaching out to You today, Lord. . .

Winning Favor

*Obviously, I'm not trying to win the approval of
people, but of God. If pleasing people were
my goal, I would not be Christ's servant.*
GALATIANS 1:10 NLT

You are so busy seeking to win the favor of your fellow humans that you have forgotten to consult with Me. And now you are anxious, worried, spent, stressed, overwrought. For, as it turns out, and as you have learned time and time again, it is impossible to please people! Believe Me! I know! And when you try to please people, you will find yourself serving them instead of Me. You will be led down paths you were not meant to walk. Your hands will be given tasks they were not meant to do. Your true vision will be blurred or, even worse, obstructed.

The remedy is to love others but not live to please them. Have the confidence to say no when you need to. Trust that My opinion and favor is of more value to you—in heaven and on earth. Have faith that I am the only One who can care for you, provide for you, unconditionally love you, prepare you, and lead you in the way you are to go. Pray; please only Me. Win My favor—and you will have the true victory!

I *desire* to please You and You only, Lord Jesus. . .

Your Pathway

The steps of a [good] man are directed and established by the Lord when He delights in his way [and He busies Himself with his every step]. Though he falls, he shall not be utterly cast down, for the Lord grasps his hand in support and upholds him.

PSALM 37:23–24 AMPC

I not only tell you where and how to walk; I make the actual pathway on which you trod. Every moment of your life, I am watching. Every time you misstep, I reroute you. Even if you take a fall, I am there to reach out and grab your hand, help you to get your balance and stand straight again.

Thus there is nowhere you can go that's out of My province. So look to Me for direction. Consult Me at every crossroads. Ask Me what lies ahead, and I will show you—because I have already gone ahead to check things out.

When you are walking in My will, My heart soars! I am thrilled with the possibilities, the opportunities that you will soon encounter. So ask Me every step of the way. As a sailor relies on the stars, you can rely on Me. I will help you navigate, even through the dark days of sorrow, grief, pain, and worry.

Peace be with you on the path I have provided.

Heavenly Father, I want to follow the path
You've provided for me. . .

....

....

....

....

....

....

....

....

....

....

....

....

....

....

....

....

....

....

....

....

....

....

Newfound Wisdom

*Trust in the L*ORD *with all your heart, and lean
not on your own understanding; in all your ways
acknowledge Him, and He shall direct your paths.*
PROVERBS 3:5–6 NKJV

I have formed you and the world you now live in. I have the knowledge of the ages—what has been, what is, what will be. I am wisdom personified. I and My Word hold all the answers to the world's questions.

Your life presents many choices to you. Every day, decisions need to be made. Yet you look only to the world or to others in your life for the answers. Because of this you are often misled. Think on this. What questions, what decisions do you now have before you, in this very moment? What is troubling you? Now turn to Me in prayer. Look into My Word for wisdom. Then trust Me and the answers I provide. Only then ask for, reflect on, and test the counsel of others. If their advice is aligned with what I have shown you, it is sound.

When you are ready, move forward with your newfound wisdom. Know that I have set you on the right path. Rely on Me and My divine knowledge—not on your own limited understanding. Take heart. I have given you all the insight you need. Walk with courage. I am with you every step of the way. Acknowledge Me in this, and you will find the confidence to walk this path.

Lord Jesus, I need courage today. . .

....

....

....

....

....

....

....

....

....

....

....

....

....

....

....

....

....

....

....

....

....

....

Early Morning Hours

Before daybreak the next morning, Jesus got
up and went out to an isolated place to pray.
Later Simon and the others went out to find him.
MARK 1:35–36 NLT

In these early morning hours, lie still. Lie still before Me until you feel My presence approach and lie down by your side.

Let us then lie together in companionable silence where peace and contentment—Mine and yours—reign and abide, within and without. The demands of the world fade away. The hammering of life becomes a dim memory. The sounds of the birds a sweet refrain. The whoosh of wind a harmless echo. And then there is left amid our silence the comfort of the love we share, the hope we cherish, the peace we crave, alone together.

Treasure these moments. For they are but a prelude to a day we will face together, a day in which you are filled with calm, courage, and confidence. A day in which you need not worry about your strength or power, but merely allow Me to continue on with you, to work through you, in you, and with you. A day in which mountains will be moved and trees uprooted.

Hold me in Your loving arms, Father God. . .

All Is Well

Fret not yourself because of evildoers, neither be envious against those who work unrighteousness (that which is not upright or in right standing with God). For they shall soon be cut down like the grass, and wither as the green herb. . . . Wait for and expect the Lord and keep and heed His way, and He will exalt you to inherit the land; [in the end] when the wicked are cut off, you shall see it.

PSALM 37:1–2, 34 AMPC

Those who have not yet heard or wanted My message of love can cause chaos in My otherwise orderly world—and yours as well. In those times, worldly what-ifs that career around in your mind can cause you to lose your balance.

Yet I tell you, do not be dismayed at those who are not walking in the Way. Do not allow them to disrupt your purpose, your calling, your expectations. For that will only hinder your way or misdirect you from the paths I have laid out for you.

Instead, leave all to Me. I am watching. I know each person's path and purpose. Everyone will receive their due in time. It is not for you to worry about or focus on.

Simply wait for Me to work. Watch for Me, expect Me, know that your end will be well. Let that content you. For now, that's all you need to know. All is well. And all will be well.

Thank You, Father, for making all things well within my soul. . .

Far beyond Imagination

Now to Him Who, by (in consequence of) the [action of His] power that is at work within us, is able to [carry out His purpose and] do superabundantly, far over and above all that we [dare] ask or think [infinitely beyond our highest prayers, desires, thoughts, hopes, or dreams]—to Him be glory.

EPHESIANS 3:20–21 AMPC

You have an amazing power deep within you, continually working. It does not sleep when you lie down for the night. It does not grow ill when your body sickens.

No. This power needs neither sleep nor remedies. It is Me working within you, gently, deeply, constantly. Live in the fullness that this power gives you. Know that this power is endeavoring to carry out My purposes so far beyond what you ever hoped or imagined!

Do not hesitate to remember this power every moment of every day. With this in mind, you know that nothing anyone says or does can hurt you. There is no situation you cannot rise above. No problem you cannot surmount. No conflict you cannot conquer. No temptation you cannot escape from.

With Me living within you, challenges become opportunities, problems become stepping-stones, and enemies become friends. Understand this. And let this understanding absolve your anxieties, power your passion, and charge your courage. With such power, there is nothing we cannot do together.

Your power amazes me, Lord Jesus. . .

Love Is All Around

"Let me give you a new command: Love one another. In the same way I loved you, you love one another. This is how everyone will recognize that you are my disciples—when they see the love you have for each other."
JOHN 13:34–35 MSG

Love is all around you—for I am love. So look for love. Open yourself to receive love. Determine to give love.

Spend much time in My presence. For it is there that you will learn about how to love, how much it has to offer you, how much the world yearns for it. Love is like water in a dry and thirsty land. People ache for a kind word, a gentle touch, a nod of acknowledgment, a silent smile, a listening ear, a hug of compassion, a glance of understanding. These all seem such little things. Yet these little things mean so much more to a soul and spirit bereft of love.

And once you begin looking for love, signs of love will pop up all around you, amazing you, giving you joy, fueling your sense of expectation. This is Me, reminding you that I am never far away. Just a breath away.

Follow My command to love each other. And you will find, as you turn your focus from self to others, that all your worries fade away, dissipate like a low-hanging fog that meets the sun's first rays.

Open my eyes to see the love in the world, Father. . .

Master Knitter

For you created my inmost being;
you knit me together in my mother's womb.
PSALM 139:13 NIV

Too long away from time in My presence and you begin to unravel. Remember that I am the One who knit you together. I know exactly how you were made—for I created you! When you were deep within the body of another, just a seed of life, My hands formed every part of your being—body, spirit, mind, and soul. Before you took a breath or felt the sun upon your face, I was filling your lungs and growing you in the darkness. When you were a mere babe, I protected you and gave you all you needed to stand where you are today.

I am the One who grows, replenishes, strengthens, feeds, tends, and cares for you. Do not neglect the source of power you have when you abide with Me, in Me. Do not forsake the master knitter, the craftsman who knows you better than anyone in the world.

Come to Me each day—in sorrow, angst, joy, relief, anger, heartache, forgiveness, confusion, peace. Whatever mode or mood you are in, seek Me. And in doing so, you will find the Light that leads you to not only well-being, but triumph—in heaven and on earth.

Shine Your heavenly light on me today, Lord. . .

But a Child

*Truly I say to you, unless you repent (change, turn about)
and become like little children [trusting, lowly, loving,
forgiving], you can never enter the kingdom of heaven
[at all]. Whoever will humble himself therefore and
become like this little child [trusting, lowly, loving,
forgiving] is greatest in the kingdom of heaven.*
MATTHEW 18:3–4 AMPC

In My eyes, you are but a child. For I have existed since before time.
I am the Ancient of Days. So come to Me as a child, expecting the
protection, love, provision, and forgiveness every child expects
from their parents. Believe with your entire being. Be wide-eyed
at the marvelous things I am going to do in your life.

When you are frightened, run to Me, jump into My arms, knowing that here nothing can harm you. When you are unsure, come to
Me for advice, knowing I have the answers. When you are anxious,
find in Me the peace and assurance that everything I have is yours.
You need simply ask and I will provide.

And as a child mimics its parents, mimic Me. Follow in My
footsteps. For as you do so, I will give you all you need to do even
more than I did while walking on the earth. And open to you will
be the kingdom of heaven.

Heavenly Father, I trust You will provide. . .

....

....

....

....

....

....

....

....

....

....

....

....

....

....

....

....

....

....

....

....

....

....

....

....

....

....

Peace from Spirit to Spirit

I will listen [with expectancy] to what God the Lord will say, for He will speak peace to His people, to His saints (those who are in right standing with Him)—but let them not turn again to [self-confident] folly.
PSALM 85:8 AMPC

You come to Me with your prayers. You have emptied out your heart, told Me all, the supposed good as well as the bad. You have unburdened yourself as I have asked you to do.

Now wait. Listen. Hear what I have to say. Know that I will speak. My words, although they may not be exactly what you want to hear, will give you peace. They will lift up your spirit. They will give you a sense of hope, an expectation of the good things that are already in and are about to come into your life.

Yet the peace that this conversation, this speaking and listening on both sides, provides will have no staying power if you leave this place and go back to depending on yourself to meet all needs, answer all questions.

So make a fresh start. Leave your self-reliance in the dust. Stick with Me, totally depending on Me alone. And you will have the peace you so crave, the peace that brings joy, understanding, and well-being. The awesome, all-encompassing peace, given from Spirit to spirit.

Father God, thank You for fresh starts. . .

Ever Closer

*So then, whatever you desire that others would do
to and for you, even so do also to and for them,
for this is (sums up) the Law and the Prophets.*
MATTHEW 7:12 AMPC

How simple the life of My followers would be if they simply treated others as they would want to be treated. And did for others what they would like to have done for them. For this is what it is all about. This is what I have done for you.

If you lived every minute of your day with the ancient command to do unto others as you would have them do unto you in the fore-front of your mind, at the center of your heart, and left everything else up to Me, how worry-free your life would be! How at peace your mind. And what seeds you would plant, what fruit you would reap! What treasures you would store up in heaven!

Living such a life, you would be deemed not only a believer in but a doer of My words of love, one that others would look to for compassion, help, forgiveness, mercy, a listening ear. You would be one that others look at and find Me shining through.

Take one step closer today to embodying this command. Write it upon your heart. Embed it in your mind. And we will draw ever closer.

Help me to treat others well, Father. . .

....

....

....

....

....

....

....

....

....

....

....

....

....

....

....

....

....

....

....

....

....

....

Watch. Wait.

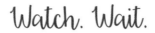

"Blessed are those who listen to me, watching daily at my doors, waiting at my doorway. For those who find me find life and receive favor from the LORD."

PROVERBS 8:34–35 NIV

You are so diverted and distraught by worldly events. You are waylaid by slights from others and weighed down by your own missteps. All these things don't just keep you from doing your kingdom work. They keep you distracted while in—or completely away from—My presence.

The remedy is to spend quality time with Me. Go to My Word and read the things I have said to My followers, the words that came directly from My very lips. Make them part of your very consciousness. Live and breathe them until they are a part of your core, your solid foundation. Embed My words in your mind so that when darts of doubt arise, you have a shield of faith to protect you from all misgivings.

You are My hands, feet, heart, and mouthpiece. Become strong. Stand for Me. Love others beyond measure. Look for Me in all. Come to Me now. Stand at My doorway, your heart in hand. Enter into My presence. Drift back into Me. Get ready to listen, to receive, then watch. Wait. I will do the rest. I will tell you all.

Rid my world of distractions, Lord Jesus. . .

A Marvelous Day

*This is from the Lord and is His doing; it is marvelous
in our eyes. This is the day which the Lord has
brought about; we will rejoice and be glad in it.*
PSALM 118:23–24 AMPC

Thank Me for this day. May it be one in which My light shines through you. One in which you are a conduit of My love, joy, grace, mercy, and forgiveness—to not only others but yourself as well.

This day is in My hands. It is all My doing. Take it as such. Celebrate it as such. Do not allow the day's events to shake you. Instead, when a challenge arises, look to Me and ask, "Yes, Lord? What would You have me do here? What would You have me say?" Then listen. When you have gotten a response, do not delay to carry out the task, to speak the words I have assigned.

Expect wonderful things to be seen, heard, revealed. Look for My hand in all. Trust that I am with you every step of the way.

Look to help those to whom I guide you. On this and every day you are able, seek to show love to someone you encounter upon your pathway. Even if it's only a smile, a nod of recognition, an understanding response, lead with compassion. Make this day I have given you not only a gift for yourself but marvelous in the eyes of another, one at the end of which you may both rejoice.

Heavenly Father, today is marvelous. . .

A Life Revived

Turn away my eyes from looking at worthless things,
and revive me in Your way. . . . I will never forget
Your precepts, for by them You have given me life.
PSALM 119:37, 93 NKJV

The more time you spend with Me, the more you grow to know Me—and the newer your life becomes each and every day. You will become wiser, for you will know what I would have you do. And when you obey My precepts, My commandments, when you do what I would have you do, whether you understand it or not and without question, you will find yourself living in a whole new and spectacular world!

Be like a child on her father's knees, obeying Me because I say so. Choose a life of faithfulness. Cling to what I have told you. Be a part of My story. Live from a God-perspective. Walk within the light that I bring into every nook and cranny of your existence. Meditate on what I have told you. Bathe yourself in the Word. And you will begin to see all things through My eyes. Worry will vanish. Misgivings dissipate. Moments of panic disappear.

In this new life, a life revived by the power and Spirit of God, nothing but peace, confidence, courage, and hope will prevail. For I will be at the heart of it—and you.

Lord, I thank You for new life. . .

....
....
....
....
....
....
....
....
....
....
....
....
....
....
....
....
....
....

A Wonder-Filled Day

My child, eat honey, for it is good, and the honeycomb is sweet to the taste. In the same way, wisdom is sweet to your soul. If you find it, you will have a bright future, and your hopes will not be cut short.
PROVERBS 24:13–14 NLT

I have in My hand not only your todays but your tomorrows as well. So do not despair over your future, do not agonize over what may happen in the days ahead. Instead, focus your energy and thoughts on today and the task I have brought to your hand.

This is how you have been made, to only concern yourself with the moment before you. Leave all else in My hands. In this way, you will have peace of mind and heart. And you will be a better and more creative laborer for Me and My kingdom. You will be freed up to see possibilities that you never glimpsed before. Your hopes and dreams will acquire a freshness brought about by the new ease you feel.

Relax. I've got everything under control. Know that I have already gone before you and cleared your pathway. Allow this new wisdom to reenergize you, to keep you moving forward and making progress in the Way. Seek the blessings of this moment, confident of a bright and hope-filled tomorrow. Have an amazing and wonder-filled day.

Lord Jesus, I won't worry about tomorrow. . .

Scripture Index